OUR
GREEN
CITY

Tanya Lloyd Kyi & Colleen Larmour

Kids Can Press

Good morning! Welcome to our green city. There are trees and flowers everywhere. Being green means we take care of all living things. People, plants and animals, too.

Can you wave to our neighbors?

When it's time for school, work or play, people move around in many ways. We drive, scooter, catch the bus, take the train or ride our bikes.

SCHOOL BUS

How many wheels
can you count?

A rain garden collects a morning shower. The pebble stream whisks away extra water — but there's still some left for splashing!

Who is hiding from the raindrops?

Even when the breeze is cool, solar panels catch the sun. Pipes gather heat from underground. Windmill blades turn above the hill. There are all sorts of ways to power our green city.

Let's play outside! What should
we do on this windy day?

These backyard farmers feed their hens and tend the beehives. Their flower beds are bright and sweet, attracting bees, birds and butterflies.

Can you spot a special visitor sipping from the zinnias?

A city can be green inside and out. While this creative bunch makes lunch, peek around their space.

Can you find five different vegetables
and five types of fruit?

Market

Thrifty Threads

THE **Refill** SHOP

LOST

CAB

Truck driver, shopkeeper, urban planner, engineer. Lots of people work together to make a green city.

PRE-LOVED FURNITURE

Seasons Cafe

Do you see ways that you can help?

In our green classroom, we plant seeds and watch our flowers grow.

We build and paint.

EARTH CAFE

We count and create.

1 2 3 4 5 6

Some days we learn things on the run. But quiet and still are also fun.

Can you spot something fast and something very slow?

We'll have new neighbors soon. Their building has a courtyard where the kids can play, and a garden on the roof! Leafy trees keep everything shady and cool.

Uh-oh, a worker has lost her hammer!
Can you see it anywhere?

A green city has many places to explore.

There are tree forts
and tiny libraries ...

BOOKS

sandboxes and
splashing fountains.

While these kids are spinning, swinging and climbing, who's peeking from the tree?

People buy food at farmers' markets and neighborhood shops. We grow our favorites in community plots. Everyone's eager to trade and share!

There's a bit of extra space in our garden.
What would you plant there?

Shhh ... can you hear the trickle of water?
Sometimes, green cities can be blue.

A heron hides among the reeds,
and frogs hop along the banks.

Who else lives in and around this stream?

There's a block party tonight. Neighbors barbecue,
share music and pass the ball down the street. Score!

You're invited to the party, too.
What games will you play?

Goodnight, city. It's time to sleep.
The lights are dimmed and the houses quiet.
The streets are still ... almost.

Can you dream of
a green tomorrow?

More Ways to Be Green

This backyard is a miniature green city, all in itself. Even a windowsill can be a garden. Do you have a space where you can be green?

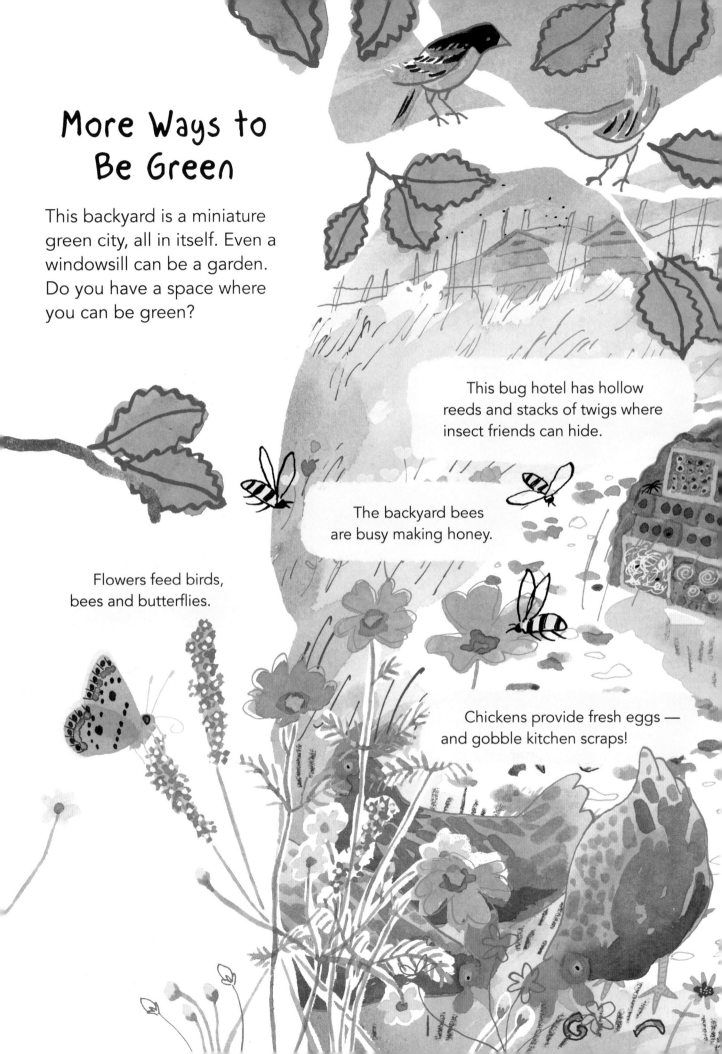

This bug hotel has hollow reeds and stacks of twigs where insect friends can hide.

The backyard bees are busy making honey.

Flowers feed birds, bees and butterflies.

Chickens provide fresh eggs — and gobble kitchen scraps!

For my friend Joanna — T.L.K.
For Glenn, with love — C.L.

Published in Canada and the U.S. by Kids Can Press Ltd.
25 Dockside Drive, Toronto, ON M5A 0B5

Kids Can Press is a Corus Entertainment Inc. company.

www.kidscanpress.com

The artwork in this book was rendered in watercolor, pen and ink and finished digitally.
The text is set in Mechanical Pencil.

Edited by Jennifer Stokes and Kathleen Keenan
Designed by Andrew Dupuis

Printed and bound in Shenzhen, China, in 10/2021 by C & C Offset

CM 22 0 9 8 7 6 5 4 3 2 1

Library and Archives Canada Cataloguing in Publication

Title: Our green city / Tanya Lloyd Kyi, Colleen Larmour.
Names: Kyi, Tanya Lloyd, 1973– author. | Larmour, Colleen, illustrator.
Description: Written by Tanya Lloyd Kyi and illustrated by Colleen Larmour.
Identifiers: Canadiana 20210197986 | ISBN 9781525304385 (hardcover)
Subjects: LCSH: Urban ecology (Sociology) — Juvenile literature. |
LCSH: Sustainable urban Development — Juvenile literature. |
LCSH: City planning — Environmental aspects — Juvenile literature. |
LCSH: Sustainable living — Juvenile literature.
Classification: LCC HT241 .K95 2022 | DDC j307.76 — dc23

Kids Can Press gratefully acknowledges that the land on which our office is located is the traditional territory of many nations, including the Mississaugas of the Credit, the Anishnabeg, the Chippewa, the Haudenosaunee and the Wendat peoples, and is now home to many diverse First Nations, Inuit and Métis peoples.

We thank the Government of Ontario, through Ontario Creates; the Ontario Arts Council; the Canada Council for the Arts; and the Government of Canada for supporting our publishing activity.

FSC
www.fsc.org
MIX
Paper from responsible sources
FSC® C008047